AF583271

SIN

THE WORLD'S UNCLEAR AND PRESENT DANGER

DALE MCNEAL

DALE & KIM MCNEAL

PUBLICATIONS

Contact info: dalepreach@aol.com

Scripture quotations, unless otherwise indicated, are taken from the Holy Bible, King James Version. All contact information listed herein are accurate at the time of publication but may change in the future or cease to exist.

To the preachers and teachers of the Gospel of Jesus Christ, servants of the Word who continue to be instant in season and out of season, preaching the Word of God. May the Lord grant double honor to you!

CONTENTS

ACKNOWLEDGMENTS

A special thanks to my friend and wife Kimberly McNeal for thirty-five years for her continued love and support of all my endeavors. To God be the Glory for the things He has done! And to Jesus Christ, the King of kings and Lord of lords. To Him that loved us and washed us from our sins in His own blood. Bless you Jesus! Amen! And to the Holy Spirit who empowers us to resist sin.

INTRODUCTION

Sin is not an easy topic to discuss in our day and age. One reason is that sin like death, is a very unpleasant subject. Because we do not like to think of ourselves as bad, or evil, or corrupt persons. Yet the Bible teaches us that this is who we are by nature.

"Behold, I was shaped in iniquity, and IN SIN did my mother conceive me." Psalms 51:5

This is one of many texts proving that we were born in sin. Some think of sin as a foreign concept, blaming the problems of society on unwholesome environments rather than on sinful humans. Therefore, a sense of guilt has become uncommon because most believe that if our actions do not harm humans, there is no reason to feel guilt or remorse. But the scripture says,

"For all have sinned and fallen short of the glory of God." Romans 3:23

Our view of the nature of God influences our understanding of sin. If we as humans were intended to reflect the nature of God which is, love, kindness, mercy, and forgiveness, and he expects all humans to be as he is, then the slightest deviation from his holy and lofty standard is sin, which leaves the human condition in serious danger. A human is not to be judged by comparison with other humans, but by conformity with God's standard. Any failure to meet that standard is sin. Man rejects God's way and chooses his own pleasures, his own success, only to find that the self-centered life has forfeited all the values it sought to conserve. Sin carries with it a built-in destruction. But the modern human being does not think deeply about these matters. They see themselves as remarkable decent citizens. They have manufactured a complacent god to replace the God who insists on morality, so they dismiss the teachings of the Bible. They are not deeply concerned about sin let alone their punishment because of sin. It is unclear to man that his plight is serious not only because of what he does, but also because of who he is, A SINNER BY NATURE AS WELL AS BY CHOICE. God is a righteous God, and he demands righteousness in his people. This righteousness is made possible by Jesus Christ! **Nevertheless, Sin against Him is a grim and dreadful affair. And we cannot begin to understand the salvation of God until we understand that Sin is the unclear and present danger.**

CHAPTER 1

WHAT IS SIN?

Sin is the transgression of the law. 1 John 3:4b

The standard against which sin can be judged is the law of God. Sin is defined as lawlessness. A defection from any of God's standards. Sin is that which is directed against God. All sin is ultimately against God (Psalm 51:4; Romans 8:7).

The Hebrew and Greek words used for sin in the pages of Scripture mean "to miss, or to fail to hit the mark," and thus "to err from a rule or law." This biblical concept comes from a study of words used in both the Old and New Testaments. The terms are numerous and together they form the basic concept of sin. From a word study we can draw certain conclusions about the Old Testament teaching on sin.

Exodus 20:20 states: "And Moses said unto the people, fear not, for God is come to prove you, and that His fear may be before your faces, that you sin not."

The word sin here is **Chata**, its basic meaning is to miss the mark, be guilty.

In Genesis 3:5 which says, For God does know that in the day you eat thereof, then your eyes shall be opened, and you shall be as gods knowing good and evil."

Evil here is the Hebrew word **ra**, meaning bad or evil. Also, this word carries the basic meaning of breaking up, or to spoil, ruin. In Isaiah 45:7 God is said to form the light and create darkness, to make peace and create evil. This is an indication that all things, including evil, are included in the plan of God, though the responsibility for committing sin rests on humanity, not on God.

Another word is **pasha**, coming from Isaiah 1:2, "Hear O heavens, and give ear, O earth, for the Lord have spoken, I have nourished and brought up children, and they have rebelled against me." Pasha means to revolt, rebellion, sin against lawful authority.

The New Testament uses words that also describes sin. Here are a few.

Anomos which is often translated, iniquity, the word means lawlessness. Breaking the law in the broadest sense (Matthew 13:41, 24:12; 1 Timothy 1:9). The Antichrist is referred to as the lawless one (2 Thessalonians 2:8).

Asebes meaning godless, this word appears mostly in 2 Peter and Jude, meaning godless apostates. Those who are unsaved are designated as ungodly (Romans 4:5,5:6).

Hamartia is the most frequently used word for sin.

When an inclusive word wanted to be use for sin, this one was used. As in the Old Testament the word means missing the mark. Many conclusions may be drawn from the New Testament word study, but all sin is a positive rebellion against God and a transgression of His standards. The prophet Habakkuk told us how terrible sin is in the sight of a holy God.

"Thine eyes are too pure to approve evil, and thou can not look on wickedness with favor" (Habakkuk 1:13).

THE OUTBREAK

To understand how the outbreak of this pandemic disease we call sin began; we must go back to its origin in Genesis the third chapter.

"Now the serpent was more subtil than any beast of the field which the Lord God had made. And he said to the woman, *yes*, hath God said, you shall not eat of every tree of the garden? And the woman said unto the serpent, we may eat of the fruit of the trees of the garden, but of the fruit of the tree, which is in the midst of the garden, God have said you shall not eat of it neither shall you touch it, lest you die. And the serpent said unto the woman, you shall not surely die for God does know that in the day you eat thereof, then your eyes shall be opened, and you shall be as gods, knowing good and evil. And when the woman saw that the tree was good for food, and that it was pleasant to the eyes and a tree to be desired to make one wise, she took of the fruit thereof, and did eat, and gave also unto her husband with her, and he did eat."

The pivotal character I want to focus on is the serpent. The Hebrew word for serpent is *nachash*. Which means serpent but the word also means to hiss, i.e., whisper a (magic) spell, to divine. Divination refers to communication with the supernatural world. A diviner in the ancient world was one who foretold omens or gave out divine information (oracles). We can see that element in this story. Eve is getting information from this being. The serpent is more than just a mere snake. He is the adversary dispensing divine information using it to provoke Eve. Like an injection when a snake bites its victim. A king cobra can control how much venom they release through its hypothermic fangs and into its victim. At times, it can release none. Because venom is valuable to a snake. He gives her an oracle or an omen, "you shall not die. God knows when you eat you will be like gods." That is, divine knowledge. The serpent's assurance and the high expectation it raised prompted Eve to look at the tree, and the longer she looked, the more she became enchanted with its fruit. Finally, she took of the fruit, ate it, and gave to her husband, and he ate. Here we see the infiltration of a spiritual superterrestrial power. As revelation unfolds, the depths of the darkness come out. The venom is at work producing the outbreak, sin.

Though seemingly innocent in the beginning, sin in its basic nature and power only becomes known in the course of history. Only gradually in the course of the history of revelation, does the spiritual power emerge that hid behind the appearance and seductive activity of the serpent. Then we learn that in the struggle of evil on earth there is also a contest of spirits and that humanity, and the world are the spoils for which the war between God and Satan, between heaven and hell, is waged.

All the power of sin on earth relates to a kingdom of darkness in the world of spirits. There too, a fall has occurred. According to Scripture, sin did not first start on earth but in heaven. Sin first broke out in the realm of spirits; it arose in the heart of creatures we have little knowledge about.

In John 8:44, Jesus states that the devil was a murderer from the beginning and abode not in the truth, because there is no truth in him. When he speaks a lie, he speaks of his own: for he is a liar and the father of it.

First John 3:8 states:

He that commits sin is of the devil; for the devil sinned FROM THE BEGINNING.

Pride took possession of him to make him strive for another and higher position.

Isaiah 14:13-15 we read,

For thou have said in thine heart, I will ascend into heaven, I will exalt my throne above the stars of God, I will sit also upon the mount of the congregation, in the sides of the north. I will ascend above the heights of the clouds; I will be like the most High. Yet thou shall be brought down to hell, to the sides of the pit.

Which resulted in his fall along with his angels. Satan is the adversary, the tempter, that ancient serpent, the originator of sin and the murderer of humanity. He beguiled Eve and sin entered the world and death by sin. The fall of man constitutes an indestructible component of the world, sin. The fall of humankind according to Scripture, was such a serious and appalling fact that the consequences of it continue to have their effect in the history of humanity to the present.

As a result of the fall, we see changes in circumstances was ushered in (the pangs of childbirth, the curse on the earth, the expulsion from the garden). Then we notice the moral reversal that took place in Adam and his descendants. After the evil was done, shame and fear took possession of them, a sense of guilt awaken in them, and they fled from the presence of God.

By one man sin entered the world, and death by sin and so death passed upon all men, for that all have sinned. (Romans 5:12). **The entire world tested positive for sin.**

This Scripture is explicit, punishment is laid upon all because of that first sin, proving that the guilt of the fall is indeed imputed. Sin ruined the entire creation, converting its righteousness into guilt, its holiness into impurity, its glory into shame, its blessedness into misery, its harmony into disorder, and its light into darkness.

"But scholars from prehistoric studies teaches that the further we go back into the past, the more we find people who lived in the most primitive state and with no culture. Human beings seem to have gradually evolved from the animal world, so that with reference to the past as well as to the present one can only speak of progress. Paradise lies ahead of us, not behind us. We have emerged from darkness and are progressively moving in the direction of light, and life, peace, and happiness."

The reverse is the case! Sin took man from the Garden of Eden to destruction. Genesis the third chapter is the story of paradise lost. The first sin was the transgression of the command not to eat of the tree of the knowledge of good and evil. That was the positive statute, it tested the obedience of Adam and Evil. And to disobey it was to disregard the authority of God and involved disobedience of all law. The first sin, the sin for which our human ancestors are responsible, has had devastating consequences for them as well as all their descendants and unleashed a flood of misery on humanity.

Consequently, humanity, every person, is burden with guilt, defiled, and subject to ruin and death. Sin is the suicidal action of the human will. Sin is now the barrier to the relationship between God and humans, thus, bringing them under God's judgment and condemnation. Sin resulted in alienation from God (Ephesians 4:18). Sin results is death. This death is physical, spiritual, and eternal. Physical death meaning the termination of human existence in the body or materialized state. Spiritual death is the separation from God. Scriptures frequently states that people apart from Jesus are dead in trespasses and sins. Eternal death is eternal separation from God. This is spoken of as the second death (Revelation 20:14). The lake of fire is the permanent state of those who chose a life of sin.

The potential of death was within creation from the beginning, but so was eternal life. Sin, in the case of Adam, and each of us, means that death is no longer merely potential but actual. The ancient serpent's venom contaminated all of humanity.

CHAPTER 2

THE SPREAD

After the fall, the Scriptures traces how sin spread and expanded in humans. And as a result, brought the judgment of God and death in some cases. The punishment of sin was not administered immediately after the fall.

"Because sentence against an evil work is not executed speedily, therefore the heart of the sons of men is fully set in them to do evil. Though a sinner does evil a hundred times, and his days be prolonged, Ecclesiastes 8:11,12.

The punishment does not go into effect fully even now only until after the final judgment (Matthew 25:41,46). God delayed and moderated sin's punishment of death to make the continuation of human life and history possible. Punishment flows from sin itself. To a degree, the history of the world is the judgment of the world. Also, God visits this world with concrete and specific punishments in addition to natural punishments. This is not an exhausted study but just a few examples of the spread of sin and its consequences.

Cain killed his brother Abel, and his blood cried out to God from the ground. Cain was sentenced as a fugitive and a vagabond. He said that his punishment was greater than he could bear. (Genesis 4:10-14).

And God saw that the wickedness of man was great in the earth, and that every imagination of the thoughts of his heart was only evil continually.

The earth was also corrupt before God, and the earth was filled with violence. And God looked upon the earth, and behold, it was corrupt, for all flesh had corrupted his way upon the earth. Finally reaching a peak that it necessitated the judgment of the flood (Genesis 6:5, 11-13).

God surveys Sodom and Gomorrah because their cry have come up to him and because their sin was very grievous and he destroyed those cities (Genesis 18:20, 21, 24, 25, 28).

In the book of Judges, it states: "and the children of Israel did evil again in the sight of the Lord" and each time the Lord caused them to go into captivity to other nations (Judges 3:12, 4:1, 6:1, 13:1,). It is God who determines the measure of the punishment by the nature of the offense. He repays everyone according to his or her deeds,

Also, unto thee, O Lord, belongs mercy for you render to every man according to his work. (Psalm 62:12)

And shall not he render to every man according to his works? (Proverbs 24:12)

And then he shall reward every man according to his works. (Matthew 16:27b)

Who will render to every man according to his deeds. (Romans 2:6)

And behold, I come quickly, and my reward is with me, to give to every man according as his work shall be (Revelation 22:12).

As sin spreads, we can see the extensiveness of it. God has characterized man's heart as being evil from childhood even after the flood (Genesis 8:21). All humans without exception, are sinners. "They are corrupt, they have done abominable works, there is none that does good.... They are all gone aside, they are all together become filthy, there is none that does good, no, not one" (Psalm 14:1,3).

"Most men will proclaim everyone his own goodness but a faithful man who can find?"

"Who can say, I have made my heart clean, I am pure from my sin?" (Proverbs 20:6,9)

Between these two rhetorical questions, the extent of human sinfulness is found. Apparently, no one can claim credit for being righteous before God. David even said, "do not bring your servant into judgment, for no one living is righteous before you" (Psalm 143:2). The same idea is implied in Psalm 130:3: "If you O Lord, kept a record of sins, O Lord, who could stand?" The preacher of Ecclesiastes says, "There is not a righteous man on earth who does what is right and never sins" (Ecclesiastes 7:20). Here in the Old Testament, there is an acknowledging of the universal sinfulness of humanity.

Even those who are specifically described as perfect have shortcomings, like Job. He refers to his sins, “Surely then you will count my steps but not keep track of my sin.”

“My offenses will be sealed up in a bag, you will cover my sin” (Job 14:16,17). Abraham was a man of great faith, yet his actions prove that he was not sinless. He demonstrated a lack of integrity twice presenting his wife Sarah as his sister (Genesis 12, 20). David was a man after God’s own heart (1 Samuel 13:14). Yet his sins were grievous, and he acknowledged them in his prayer of repentance in Psalm 51. In Isaiah 6 we find the prophet standing before the throne of God, seeing the seraphims with face and feet covered each with six wings calling out to one another, Holy, holy, holy is the Lord of hosts: the earth is filled with his glory.

The prophet Isaiah said, Woe is me! For I am undone! Because I am a man of unclean lips, and I dwell in the midst of a people of unclean lips, for my eyes have seen the King, the Lord of hosts. Then flew one of the seraphims unto me, having a live coal in his hand, which he had taken with the tongs from off the altar. And he laid it upon my mouth and said, Lo, this have touched your lips, and your iniquity is taken away, and your sin purged.”

Again, the prophet recognized his sin in the presence of God. And that is how we know when a person is getting close to God. The closer you get to God, the more disgusted you become with yourself. The more you begin to see yourself. This is the Old Testament; the New Testament is even clearer concerning the universality of human sin. Romans the third chapter verses 9-12 says,

"What then? Are we better than they? No, in no wise: for we have before proved both Jews and Gentiles, that they are all under sin. As it is written, there is none righteous, no not one. There is none that understands, there is none that seek after God. They are all gone out of the way, they are together become unprofitable. There is none that do good, no, not one."

Paul makes it plain that he is not only talking about unbelievers, but believers as well, including himself. He says in verse twenty-three, "ALL HAVE SINNED, AND COME SHORT OF THE GLORY OF GOD." He acknowledges that all of us lived as a son of disobedience or lived among them at one time, gratifying the cravings of our sinful nature and following its desires and thoughts. And like the rest, we were by nature objects of wrath (Ephesians 2:3). The Scripture has concluded that all are under sin (Galatians 3:22). The same is true in 1 John 5:19 indicating that "the whole world is under the control of the evil one."

Having seen that the spread of sin is universal, we turn to the issue of how it unleashed a flood of misery on humanity. Subjecting everyone to the penalty of sin, which is death. "The wages of sin is death." Therefore, just as sin entered the world through one man, and death through sin, and in this way, death came to all men, because all sinned (Romans 5:12). Again, here too, sin is considered universal.

Since the expulsion of humanity meant death passed to all humanity because of Adam's sin, death and the serpent became associated with each other in biblical thought. Darkness, disease, death, and chaos become part of that association.

The curses that followed the events in the garden bound the fate of humanity together with the seed of the serpent, all those who oppose the rule of God in either the earthly or the spiritual realm. Jesus called the Pharisees, "serpents" and "offspring of vipers" (Matthew 23:33) describing people whose lives are characterized by wickedness as "children of the devil."

Despite the snake's beguiling beauty, they posed a genuine danger. Snakes often strike from hiding, biting without warning. This ever-present danger serves as a metaphor of sudden judgment. The snake (the devil) is an agent of chaos, a member of the destructive forces that continually attempt to tear apart the fabric of creation. The virus of sin is here and like any infective agent, is too small to be seen but can multiply only within the living cells of a host. Because viruses can multiply only inside infected cells, they are not considered to be alive. And because sin is growing in those already infected, most do not believe sin is alive.

CHAPTER 3

THE PANDEMIC

Sin is a serious matter involving dire consequences. Men may not be deeply concerned about it, but God is. It is seen in the recognition that the ministry of Jesus is "to them which sat in the region and shadow of death" Matthew 4:16. Wherever sin is present, the presence of death is sensed. People are in mortal danger making them the objects of his mission. In the Gospels, Jesus accepts universal sinfulness as something that can be taken for granted. In Matthew 7:11, speaking about men's charitable deeds He says, "if you then, being evil know how to give good gifts to your children..." notice how "being evil" is slipped in. It does not need to be argued, it can be assumed. But if Jesus is sure that men are naturally sinful, He is not complacent about the consequences. There is a such thing as the judgment. There is a such thing as hell fire Matthew 5:21,22. This is the pandemic sin has caused around the entire world.

This pandemic is so serious that Jesus said the loss of a foot, or an eye is to be preferred to hell fire,

And if your foot offends you, cut it off it is better for you to enter halt into life than having two feet to be cast into hell, into the fire that never shall be quenched. Mark 9:45

And if your right eye offends you, pluck it out and cast it from you, for it is profitable for you that one of your members should perish and not that your whole body should be cast into hell. Matthew 5:29

Again, the pandemic of sin is so serious that Jesus is telling us that the amputation of the infected parts of the body should be preferred and discarded and enter life (heaven) maimed than to keep those infected members of the body and have the whole body cast into hell fire. Understand that this virus called sin causes surgical removal one way or another. Of another sinner Jesus said that it would be better for him to have a millstone tied about his neck and be cast into the sea than to have committed his sin **Matthew 18:6.** In reference to the sin of Judas, Jesus said, good were it for that man if he had not been born **Matthew 26:24, Mark 14:21.**

The results of sin in the bible are regarded with horror. It is horrible and it is horrible in its consequences. The deaths of Ananias and Sapphira made a profound impression on the infant church. This was a punishment not of the heathen but of believers **Acts 5:1-11.** They had no special immunity. All sin, wherever found, is a horrible thing. Its punishment, whether in the here and now or in the hereafter, is certain and severe.

Paul the Apostle sees all men as sinners; this means that the wrath of God must be expected to be directed against all men. **Ephesians 2:3** says that by nature we all are children of wrath. God's wrath comes upon "the sons of disobedience" **Ephesians 5:6, Colossians 3:6.** This wrath is not exhausted in this life, because Paul speaks of the "wrath to come" **1 Thessalonians 1:10.**

Paul also speaks of men as "alienated" from God **(Ephesians 4:18)** or as "enemies" of God **(Romans 5:10).** These expressions do not mean that there is a coolness between God and sinners. They mean that they are in opposition. God leaves no room for complacency.

"Sin that it might be shown to be sin, by working death to me" Romans 7:13. Sin has results which are inescapable and among them is death. The pandemic of sin brings death. Modern people often have a shallow view of life and are not disturbed by it. They do not see themselves as being in any real danger and therefore see no need of salvation. This also constitutes a threat and if life is like this, humanity is in grave and imminent danger. Even some of God's people. A continuing emphasis on the love of God to this generation makes some unaware and unmindful of their danger at the judgment of God. An over emphasis on love to people do nothing but increase their complacency. I am not saying that the love of God is unimportant I am saying that most are unaware that the biblical narrative is heavy with impending judgment. **"Behold therefore the goodness and severity of God" Romans 11:22.**

The scripture says, **"it is a fearful thing to fall into the hands of the living God" Hebrews 10:31.** We shall stand before God and face a serious reckoning for what we have done and what we have not done. And because we shall one day stand before Him, we do well to give heed to the situation in which our sin has placed us.

O wretched man that I am! Who shall deliver me from the body of this death?

THE ANTIDOTE

The remedy to counteract the effects of poison from the serpent's venom and humanity's disobedience is God's antidote, Jesus Christ! God brings men salvation through the death of Christ.

But we see Jesus.... that he by the grace of God should taste death for every man. Hebrews 2:9

That is what it costs God to deal with man's sin. "To create the heavens and the earth costs him no labor, no anguish; but to take away the sin of the world costs Him His own lifeblood." [1]

Now instead of sin being the deadly pandemic causing death and destruction, God sends Jesus Christ the supernatural vaccine, the powerful serum against the serpent's venom!

The prophet Hosea declared that Jesus was our cure and our savior. He said:

"I will ransom them from the power of the GRAVE, I will redeem them from DEATH. O Death, I WILL BE YOUR PLAGUES, O GRAVE, I WILL BE YOUR DESTRUCTION!" Hosea 13:14

---

[1] Lesslie Newbigin, Sin and Salvation

Jesus is the plague against sin, against death, against diseases, and against the powers of darkness! For those who have been injected with the venom of sin, there is a cure for this pandemic. When the children of Israel sinned against God in the wilderness by speaking against God, the Lord Said to Moses,

"Make a snake and put it up on a pole, anyone who is bitten can look at it and live. So, Moses made a bronze snake and put it up on a pole. Then when anyone was bitten by a snake and looked at the bronze snake, they lived." Numbers 21:8,9

Jesus said, as Moses lifted the serpent in the wilderness, even so He must be lifted up (John 3:14). Anyone who looks to Jesus will live! He provides the cure for man's rebellion and the serpent's bite.

Because he was wounded for our transgressions, he was bruised for our iniquities, and upon him was the chastisement that made us whole, and with his stripes we are healed.

And the Lord has laid on Him the iniquity of us all Isaiah 53:5, 6b. (RSV)

Through His death He destroyed him who had the power of death, that is, the devil (Hebrews 2:14). By His cross peace has been secured with God, Colossians 2:14. If anyone would be saved, they must look to the savior and follow Him. Confess your sins, repent, and believe the Gospel of Jesus Christ. Believe that he died for the sins of humanity. Or you will never escape the pandemic of sin unto death.

"He that believes on the Son (Jesus) have eternal life; but he that obey not the Son shall not see life, but the wrath of God abides on him" John 3:36.

In flaming fire taking vengeance on them that know not God, and that obey not the gospel of our Lord Jesus Christ. Who shall be punished with everlasting destruction from the presence of the Lord, and from the glory of His power 2 Thessalonians 1:8,9.

And I saw a great white throne, and Him that sat on it, from whose face the earth and the heaven fled away, and there was found no place for them. And I saw the dead, small and great stand before God, and the books were opened, and another book was opened, which is the book of life, and the dead were judged out of those things which were written in the books, according to their works. And the sea gave up the dead which were in it, and death and hell delivered up the dead which were in them. And they were judged every man according to their works. And death and hell were cast into the lake of fire. This is the second death.

AND WHOSOEVER WAS NOT FOUND WRITTEN IN THE BOOK OF LIFE WAS CAST INTO THE LAKE OF FIRE. REVELATION 20:11-15.

Jesus Christ is the only answer. For God so loved the world that he gave His only begotten Son to die for our sins. He took our place and died on the cross to save us from the wrath to come, to reconcile us back to God, and to give us eternal life.

It is important that you get born again, that you get saved or you will never reach heaven or escape the wrath to come. How shall we escape if we neglect so great salvation?

Ask God to forgive you of your sins and receive Jesus in your heart by asking Him to save you. Ask Him to wash you in His blood, tell God that you believe Jesus died for your sins and that His Resurrection was for your justification, and if you do this then according to Word of God you are now saved! Welcome to the family of God!

www.ingramcontent.com/pod-product-compliance
Lightning Source LLC
LaVergne TN
LVHW021313160826
845679LV00001B/330

* 9 7 9 8 8 4 2 6 1 3 8 5 4 *